as steam

rises

David Michael Lippman

Printed in the United States of America

Published by Soul-Care Press Inc.

Soul-Care Press Inc.
Santa Cruz, California
DavidMichaelLippman.com

Cover Design: oh, hello friend & J. Edward Design
Cover Photo: Pawel Kadysz
Original Package Design: Soul-Care Press

ISBN: 978-0-9985577-0-0

First Edition

10 9 8 7 6 5 4 3 2 1

To my beautiful wife…you've taught me more about my heart than anyone else. I am so blessed to spend every morning with you.

"I would rather spend one lifetime with you than face all of the ages of this world alone."

-J.R.R.Tolkien, *The Fellowship of the Ring*

"One runs the risk of weeping a little, if one lets himself be tamed…"

-Antoine de Saint-Exupery, *The Little Prince*

"You can't see it and you know it's there only by…the hush song coming so low to your ears you fear it might be silence and you listen keen and you listen long and you know it's more than silence for you get the hush song so lovely it hurts and cuts into your heart…so you listen and while you listen you pray and after you pray you meditate, then pray more and one day it's as though a great slow wind had washed you clean and strong inside and out…"

-Carl Sandburg, *Honey & Salt*

"I said to my soul, be still, and let the dark come upon you which shall be the darkness of God…I said to my soul, be still, and wait without hope…the faith and the love and the hope are all in the waiting. Wait without thought, for you are not ready for thought: so the darkness shall be the light, and the stillness the dancing…"

-T.S. Eliot, *Four Quartets*

"But for those obstinate questionings...blank misgivings of a creature moving about in worlds not realized, high instincts through which our mortal nature did tremble like guilty thing surprised...are yet the fountain-light of all our day...and have the power to make our noisy years seem moments in the being of the eternal Silence: truths that wake to perish never."

-William Wordsworth, *Ode: Intimations of Immortality from Recollections of Early Childhood*

CONTENTS

PREFACE

This small book of poetry contemplates the ordinary and seemingly insignificant habit of sipping a cup of coffee or tea in the morning. Sometimes rushed and often underappreciated, there still remains a hidden magic behind those quiet sips. Coffee and tea are not just about caffeine or gourmet quality, but these contain an experience that can touch the inner life, a trace amount of the poet's virtue: hospitality.

Hospitality is the core gift of poetry. This gift contains a host of sub-gifts everyone longs for: compassion, understanding, acceptance, tenderness, wisdom and peace. Yet, this gift of the open, personal presence of another is fading from homes, schools, offices, churches, etc. What used to be places of connection are becoming dominated by a philosophy of production, achievement and survival. Our accomplishments and task-lists have overshadowed, even displaced, the gift of our hospitality.

In omitting this gift to others, we can also forget how to be hospitable to our own souls. It is rare today to take time to sit, quiet oneself and reflect on the vastness of one's life. Poetry, as I see it, is the written reclamation of our hearts, our core self. By engaging in authentic inner dialogue, we provide hospitality first to our own souls. This practice can open us to a vast, easily-offered hospitality toward others. The intersection of hospitality and our heart can even begin with a mug of coffee or tea on an ordinary morning.

These poems are written to evoke this sense of hospitality: an openness to the true you. In other words, home. Some may never have found a place like this where space is provided to authentically explore your heart. May this be the place for you to begin. Some of you may have been on this journey for many long years. May these words nourish your heart and strengthen your bones.

Whether you read alone or in a crowd, these poems can lead you toward deeper connection with yourself and others[1]. Though I would've loved to sit down with you and share a mug together, I cannot provide everyone the gift of physical hospitality. But I do believe you are never alone and my prayer is for this book to be a reminder to you; evidence of the posture of hospitality still alive in this world.

I encourage you, as best you can, to read this with a warm mug. Quiet yourself from the busy world. Let the words speak. Let your thoughts brew. Let your mind relax. Consider the present moment. Bring yourself to the poem. Underline your favorite parts. Linger a moment or two....

---

[1] First-time poetry readers begin with A Beginners Guide to Poetry, p 45.

And as steam rises,

may your heart learn to listen once again.

I - *sitting with you*

and i'll be sitting with you
until our mugs grow cold,
until the world settles
down around us
and all the untold stories
share dearly
like old friends,
telling of holes made of faces
soft touches, warm embraces,
the kind where the world bends in to listen
and wonder with us
what has been and what its ending is,
you and i had thought we were pretending
all the while love crept in
unnoticed and unbidden,
like the shadowy reflection in our mirror
light reflects light
until all things are clear.

II - *the open conversation*

as steam rises,
i breathe and sip
this space,
the open conversation
this world is so afraid of:
a quiet moment before
a universe-sized God, who spoke
with moses, walked with adam
and whispers still to me.
who listens
to a heart content to be
broken true and seen through
in a quiet morning, speaking
unsaid words over coffee
with the One who wrote down
my days and speaks still
in not-so-insignificant ways, weighing,
marking my soul as gold and dross.
i guess these are the moments where i count it all,
every single shard of shattered glass, as loss.

III - *home is coming close*

as steam rises
i sip warmth
flooding over lip and tongue.
steam curls by my eyes
a sign of peace to the roadweary,
and i know i'm nearly home.

sure, engines wane. sure,
aching hearts ache.
but when steam rises in the morning
as quiet surrounds,
slowing my breathing,
speaking comfort rich and white,
warm as cream darkening in my drink,
i think i'll be home soon.

for home is creeping in on me
lightly rustling in the tree then
there in the corner
                          climbing up the wall;

raindrops of hope drip from the ceiling.

gallons upon gallons slosh at my feet

and i b r e a t h e h o p e a g a i n

home. ah, yes, home.
home is coming close.

IV - *stay awhile*

a small round mug filled with golden light.
steam waves up like white flags
in the depth debris waits.
a testimony that not
all that seems like
dirt remains
unworthy
of being

called

beautiful,

coaxing a smile,
"come on,
      take a sip,
            stay awhile."

V - *under lock and key*

as steam rises
i sip and breathe
the sweet-bitter liquid.
sensations warm on my tongue
that spill down into my core.
i breathe in
opening secrets i've kept
from my own mind,
things i've promised to forget.

and with time
they remain as forgotten
as my first birthday.

waiting silent, waiting still
inside a bunker inside a hill,
hidden from a war never to begin,
listening for a sword and story
for a wounded hero
for a dance of thieves,
for a beautiful damsel
and a beggar's old, rusty key

oh, for just one echo below
from the words i've forced out,
and the words i'll never let go.

no, i've kept my secrets under lock and key,
but truth is, my secrets are keeping me.

VI - *who you share your mornings with*

as steam rises
in white curls
like fog greeting shore,
a subtle moment stilled,
calming voices unimportant, unneeded, uninvited.

in this silent hour
i can be myself.
i don't have to be anyone else.
here with my history on my shoulders
and beliefs stuffed like a lover's note
in my back pocket.

a rising fire of slow dawn
sneaks-in through words.
rising behind my eyes,
beholding unseen secrets
even the world keeps, mine
and those of another time,
shining as a spider's web on a frosty morn
touching seams gleam and reveal
a secret shared in love.

what we share
when we really share
is the most important thing about us.

with friends,
enmity becomes transparency.

in a world of made-up faces,
faux-embraces,
where voices curl like irons,
and looks can shatter like vases,

it matters more than anything else
who you share your mornings with.

VII - *a welcomed reception*

as steam rises
in curling white pirouettes,
holding hands they rise,
bend and rise,
bend and rise,
always lifting, always lilting,
as a prayer murmured on a quiet morning

turning me from daily tasks
to rise as they rise
before an hour i cannot comprehend or control.

my soul rests thin, transparent as vapor.
a breath breathed over water still as glass.

this quiet dance,

where ordinary things
like cookware, coffee, sipping;
                just another task to begin,
                but if s l o w e d,
and touched just-so, with light illumined
from places unknown,

without a word,
could open the deadlocks of the soul.

on such days
a soul begins to see things like coffee
like cookware, like morning,

like quiet words shared in heartfelt prayer;
words that rise as souls in waltz,
moving higher as unseen eyes grasp wider,
more clearly than ever
a beauty wrapped, intimate,

becoming a welcomed reception,
a communion where child and father
sip coffee together,
and really finally listen to each other
            like they've planned on for oh so long.

VIII - *the business of becoming*

soft wisps of steam
rise like a dying fire.
i sip the delicate wonder
of a single moment quiet, in the early morn.
before frenzieddesirescrowdin
asking me not so discreetly
to turn from a warm mug,
to stop thinking private thoughts,
to be hurried, productive,
just like everyone ought to, but i ask,

"whose voice is this who speaks so freely
without greeting or introducing,
interrupting a once private moment
before my cup and the day?"

no one answers.

light mist twirls up as comforting hands
strumming a quiet morning song,
that rises early and floats away
on seas of fog toward an endless dawn.
awakening where faces and voices
no longer beckon away and up, bustle and go;
    then and now, i will be as steam drawn
into unseen air, dancing as i grow.

believe me, i would rather be in the business of
    becoming
then trapped in a world of clamoring voices.

IX - *a breath infinitely breathed*

as steam rises,
a breath exhaled through winter lungs,
rising in the warmth of chest and heart,
    beat and bone,
muscles and nerves whirr and click, keeping time
like the mechanics of a sentient grandfather clock,
always tick-tocking whether i'm looking or not.

even our bodies work mindless of our will
to move or wake or sleep or walk
or breathe or die.
inner worlds
orchestrating a symphony
of consciousness and survival
work and play,
reason and faith,
distinctions cut
as a blade through union,
separating what-is from
what-ought-to-be,
splitting the now with the never-could-conceive
                and the i-just-can't-stop-worrying,

bending reality like a prism into a half-light hovel,
making body and mind sit down, not as friends,
nor companions, nor wayfarers
on the journey long,

but slaves lashed, beaten into a one-sided,
single-minded, hole-inside-my-soul

sort of regimen.
eventually even temple walls forget
the reason they stand.
hearts, souls, trapped like the ark behind a veil,
cut off from communion.
a by-word relic
only used once if twice a year.

    still hidden like the God-within it.

a great heartbeat throbs beneath all life,
longing to be upturned
in us, through us
shouting muffled psalms of praise,
shaking the foundations
of everything made and unmaking
'til quivers break open new paths
for hearts and eyes and bodies to follow.

the very fires that burn and heat such things
    as lungs, coffee and galaxies,
    burn with a fire not their own
    and shake to see worlds no longer alone,

    but entwined with divinity and desecration
    holy and the horror,
    non-fiction woven with folklore,
    creation mingling with chaos.

find and see how all life rises like steam
from a single source;

a breath infinitely breathed.

X - *my quiet morning*

as steam rises
my heart lifts with the swirls
and disappears into thin air,
slipping away like shadows in the night,
haunting ghosts of unknown origin
with familiar voices,
voices like mine.

"when you seek
you shall find,"
no comfort
in the vast
stillness
of the
soul.

no,
there's
no one here.

the pit-pat of rain
sounding drops in a tin can
rap-rapping at the cauldron door.
but it never opens, not anymore.
even ghosts won't show themselves
beneath deepest secret.

only voices. only quiet.
only lonesome.
a vast wasteland

still to be determined, defined.

no human
can garden this alone,
no. too vast. too wild.
too much to see, to overcome,
to lose.

it is here i sit
and watch white ghosts slip
from my cup like the hopes
of unknown souls, here.

in a wasteland:

my quiet morning.

XI - *the gentle knocking*

as steam rises
in translucent white,
veiling what is from what might be,
i think, i feel,
i kneel inside for the rising incomprehensible now

veiled behind prayers i can barely receive
let alone speak to ceilings,

somehow still soul-depths rise like steam,
silent, secret.

i hear a knocking down below,
a gentle rapping, a patient pause. nothing more.

a knock,
a bated silence,
an unspoken question,
then a quick distraction
and my mind returns to steam rising
and all the words i'm surmising
to express the fullness of a quiet moment like this.

but still and ever the knocking comes.
still and ever it waits
with beckoning questions.
the sort any grown man trembles to answer.

i wanted to write something beautiful.

so i keep pen fixed on page.
heart, mind, entangled, engaged;

to spite the knocking knocking,
ever waiting, often pausing,
interrupting prayers so peacefully rising
like steam off my mug.

i wanted to create a lovely longing.

but will i embrace that knocking knocking
and, ugh, that patient waiting?

i know someone's there,
just ready to wag a finger
pointing out all that's undone inside my door.

i just can't seem to shake it.

that patient wait,
that silence between,
that gentle quality of rapping rapping,
never tiring of rapping for me,
never slamming shouting or giving up,

what kind of person does this?

what kind of someone waits willingly
behind a closed door
for God-knows how long,

not seeming the least bit annoyed by my writing,
by my quiet meditations on distraction and steam
rising from ordinary things like coffee?

waiting and writing, writing and waiting.

baiting something beautiful
to come,
to rise from a mug,
to surmise in hand.

but no one in the end really cares
so much about the poetry,
but the poet.
not the words writing,
but a storied soul full of words and wordlessness.

so i put down my pen and i
turn to the door and i
stare for a moment and i
blink open eyes and i
grab the handle and i
pray in a way so long forgotten 'til i
can muster enough strength to turn
my wrist, and i
wait,
oh, do i
wait,
for the gentle one
with gentle knocks
coming to interrupt this not-so-silent morning
with my mug.

XII *- to sit in silence*

as steam rises
my eyes trace white spirals,
sparrows taking flight
s t r e t c h i n g
for the unseen,
lifting
from the dark, bitter earth.

in private i've spoken so,
with eyelids closed
and a mouthful of repentance stones,
hoping to rise.
yet here i wait
under liturgy self-made,
protocol training for an overwhelming world.
giving fear the title of religious habit,
a burning sacrifice of lip-service
to feel just a bit better.
but am i really burning here?

hiding inside an unembraced life
from what it is to truly live
with religious language.

silent, i place each stone
into unseen hands,
letting silence weigh
and weigh in on
this one-sided
conversation.

oh it's so much more convenient
not to let my heart speak.

oh it's so much more convenient
pretending not to see,

almost stealing away my inheritance:
a prodigal protecting my name
from the harsh words
falling from my lips,

if i were to really sit in silence.

XIII - *inside a quiet simple prayer*

as steam rises
i watch airwaves play like children
without inhibition,
no thread of hesitation,
always rising,
>   ever playing, ever rising
>   from a sea of silent glass.

as i sip, i breathe their fragrance
and briefly they envelop me,
then again, ever again
they rise without consequence
or second thought of who i am
or what i've given.

i consider this seriously for a moment,
and for that moment i am softened.

but somewhere deep inside
where the warm drink warms,
i know i have to carry burdens
thin wisps could never imagine.

their one job, their sole task,
their singular journey,
>   to accept the heat and rise,
>   thin as mist.
>   light entwined.
>   a meandering forgetfulness.

how often do i
breathe like them?
 how often do i meander
down lanes undiscovered
finding flowers growing
without thought of color,
or how shapely their stalk,
or whose vase they'll fill when plucked
for some beautiful city assignment?
flowers grow like steam rises, without concern
of how long their beauty will endure
or who might meander by
to finally appreciate their petals,

they seem to say:
remember the slow hour.

the hour most throw away
at the beginning of the day,
when beauty is at it's height.

that bit that makes everyday
just a bit different:
the not-so-unrequited art
of still seeing a world made beautiful

with byways forgotten,
where flowered generations grow
through tunnels known once by men
who heard not an automobile engine,
men who shepherded,
carrying packs with meals plucked,

chopped, harvested by dust-encrusted hands.

a tireless knowing of years and years
with others just like me,
sitting before a warm cup
thinking a wanderer's thoughts
traipsing through flowered fields
with no legitimate purpose whatsoever
and plucking a few to sit before
in the quiet of early morn.

oh, to be like steam,
in unforgetful-forgetfulness remembering
what is truest in this world lifting high
and higher still
until, as all true things do,
it slips into the unseen.

eyes cannot find
where hearts hide—
led by little things
like steam and flowers
toward unwinding days,
a place where home forever is wrapped together
inside a quiet simple prayer.

XIV - *quiet as the grave*

as steam rises
i breathe in the bitter sweet,
watching mahogany mingle with clouds of cream.

i sigh,
as this moment slows.
the multi-fractured days repose, bowing
as a fragrant rose unfolds,
a satisfying inner groan
of "wow"
and "thank you."

not so in me.

i am earthed.
in a kitchen.
with a pen.
and a mug.
i cannot rise
from my body
through heart
or lungs
like steam
into air
concealing things beyond dust
beyond molecules, beyond even light.

not so in me.

some say many roads lead to heaven above,

just keep it up.

but my tattered prayers
are all broken ladders
never touching heaven,
arising only from a bitter cup.

i see now
no disorder can reorient disorder.

rather,
give up the ghost.

the trade's been made
a prescription written in blood,
the bitter cup drunk to the dregs.

by whom, you ask?
 who else?

still, we pace
back and forth
wondering about an outcome?

work is waste
when an empty cup
waits, at peace.

quiet as the grave.

XV - *open chests and empty hands*

as steam rises
in long meandering chimney curls,
i cannot help but think of all that's come before
and all that still may be.

an unwinding trail of mind, unfamiliar and furled.

my poor feet ache from wandering still.
the sky thick with branches
is draped in low fogbreath.

footsteps of thought
follow hopes hollow
as rotten wood.

no bearings.
no path cleared in the veil of trees.
trudging through a dismal fray,
i find there's no balm potent as discovery:
the wandering path hides a hospital wing,
a recovery from helplessness,
a healing never fully finished.
helplessness stays
but despair dissipates.

will someday
clouds rise high like steam off a mug?
will someday sunlight illumine a path before us?
a narrow trail for wandering souls with open
chests and empty hands?

XVI - *a burden shared*

steam wisps twirl till unseen.
lifting, always lifting higher higher,
as tendrils of smoke from fire.

a poet once wrote
in the woods two roads diverge, i the wiser
followed the tugging heart
heeding warnings for boys like me:
"question, always question the beaten path"
oh how i believed.

through brambled trails i wove between
broken branches, bending reeds, bruised wicks,
hidden pockets of primrose and poison,
wondering, all the while wondering

who taught the wise these things?
and where do they call home?
yes, yes, many boys become men lost
seeking ways through forest and frost,

but i've found secret trails
aren't shortcuts or brighter days,
every path splits open wounds,
no story is invulnerable,
nothing guaranteed. all is gift.
even in abandonment no life is lived
utterly alone.

who knows, someday we may reach a clearing

and stumble upon one another, embracing.
the few of us who carried packs
sit down to kindle a fire,
pouring water,
steeping our smiles
in time spent together.

lifting a warm cup
between fingers.
a chill sets in.
we linger.
evening
comes.

we sip
and speak until
all the questions
become the companions
they have always been.

we smile as comforting sips warm our throats.
we smile as a comforting glow warms our souls.

and i recall how two roads diverged,
separate stories bringing only renewed joys
for those who hold mugs together in the evening,

speaking of intertwining things like us,
a burden shared is burden enough for both of us.

XVII - *that was almost me*

foam flecked edges
of my once-frothed mug
dry like water cracks in earth,
bringing to mind long months wandering
in waterless places,
never forgetting the ageless pain
a bitter road behind and ever with me.

dry mouthed, cotton lipped,
not a drip in my cup but
emptiness. loss.
no signs or borders.
no towns or faces.
no refuge. no oasis.

wrestling demons cloaked
in gowns of everyday.

one last torpid sip,
the fainting taste
mocks me.

after the fires died came endless cold nights
mocking stars
unknown routes
my fragile cup shaking,
begging, begging for food, water, something
anything to cool this burning day
or sooth this frostbite night.

striding as living dead
only able to lean into
the thin fragile moment.
years blurred together beyond count.
a mind wasting,
wandering as mule without a master,
no haste, no home.

foam flecked mouth dust dry
despairing of despair.

not an ounce of effort left
all spent.
longing only to long
for one new breath.

i sip now and think of it.
the bitter aroma arises
and my heart sighs

for i know now how to kill a man.
give him desire, then
drop him in a desert
with a cup as his only companion

and no one within a
hundred miles
to listen,
to watch
his wailing.

yes,
that was almost me.

XVIII - *reward*

as steam rises
i contemplate the meaning of moments
when coffee or tea
is sipped slowly,
a taste of relief
a brief ceasing of the hastening race.

a moment more
and our thoughts approach as old friends,
beckoning conversation over a warm mug,
trying on our skin,
seeing what fits about us,
learning who actually dwells within our body.

then as quiet comes
emptiness allows the unheard a voice.

silence sits in the space between our souls
and listens
to the mutterings we won't let out
the chattering of then and now,

to the something's we've called nothing's
pushed so far down
and casually dismiss as silence.

the loudest things about us
crawl beneath our skin

calling out in moments made thin

and long as a lover's whisper,
true and strong as a steel blade,
fiery and dangerous as a dragon's cave.

oh, son or daughter, friend or foe,
watch where you wander
watch where you go

in twilight quiet becomes such a friend,
in the moment of death,
in the moment of dread,
when chest is tight,
when eyes are spent,
when hope is lost,
when faith is dead.

then and ever, enter into your chambers
and close the door behind.
fold your hands
and speak in silence

your heart will bear its own reward.

XIX - *catching light*

as steam rises
caught with light,
molecules of water taking flight,
for the moment, i must close my eyes
and take in the sweet, roasted scents,
all that surrounds the anticipation
the exchange, the taste, the sounds.

and i bow
as warmth brews the bitter soul,
earth rising becoming whole,
rising in a glimmer and a shine,
then dissipating, only to rise again
more radiant, a lovely light-filled rise

catching light
upon an ordinary cup.

to the secret that fills rising steam,
to the same secret filling you and me,
receive the invitation
without questioning
consequences.
just open eyelids,
and let heat rise

you and i
catching light.

XX - *servant*

as steam rises like a breath
exhaled on a winter night,
hiding ghosts, hiding sight,
lifting thoughts as winds upon water.

over breakers over waves old men speak
of vapor souls rising and fading.
they speak of death as a friend,
to whom every man and woman
must bend.

but i fantasized instead
to shirk death's immanent mark.
to hide from any hint of pain,
believing the path for me lay in pleasant places
as long as i managed such and such,
and shifted who-knows-what
into shades where only shadows hide.

i once believed regarding death
i had choice.

but providence wouldn't have its rule broke.
everything dark and stolen inside
must. be. exposed.
coming up at night as breath,
arising as steam from a mug,
seen, then unseen, then seen again,
reminding one of the burning heat within.

i look upon these secrets rising from my mug.
as i sip, my eyes, my hands, my breath become
aware of this veiled pain,
this veiled face,
mine, and behind
the hands of another, older, sipping death for me.

calling death by a different name:
    "servant."

every porcelain glass shakes like a bell.
every vapor flip-turns
playing like a child in ocean swells.
and i almost see a smile in the mist arising
and i almost hear a voice whispering,
"this is my beloved son, listen.
listen to him…"

XXI - *quiet fire*

as steam rises
my heart abates and abides in
life and life-not-yet,

> days-may-never and an unending-forever
> kind of play.

'til a quiet fire flames
for more than, and more of,
this very moment.

who knows, for you maybe
peace comes as a soft bird searching?

or as a hammer slamming your chest stealing
wind from lungs?

or it might come, as it does for me,
like a pinching little bug,
irritatingly prodding till i turn
from the unimportant to look upon
the living soil,
the trees that guard my waking days,
the bright sky and trails?

peace feels like a pain
you run away from
yet always want more of.

a sort of private ache.

peace is hidden in my lonely morning.
peace is an absent wound.
peace, a quiet fire.
peace always, always mingled with desire.

when will peace hide no longer in aching corners?

when will peace expand to embrace
all who wake with pain on their shoulders?

who want for something true, something better,
something worth sticking around for?

XXII – *silence:peace*

as steam rises
past eyelids
floating wisps
lilt, kiss, spin into nothingness.

there peace sits
on the porch of silence
for anyone, everyone to let him in.

with an unuttered invitation
unfettered by light
dancing, lilting, kissing, rising
ever rising before blinking eyes.

childish in still waiting; childish in waiting still.

'til a secret breath, an exhaled "yes"
i embrace the boy inside my chest.

and while quiet, i see the eyes of a thousand
generations smiling at a welcomed invitation.

while quiet, i bow before this elusive moment.

while quiet, aching churns for an end.

while quiet, voices bend

and bend

and bend.

i find, in the silence while i wait,
that silence isn't so intimidating anymore.

still suspicion hides behind
question upon question,
peeking a shy face in my direction.

i wave, barely able to lift my hand,
i pray that grasping ache long forgotten
timid as a rose petal on a frosty morn.
hidden deep as bone.

i need a friend,
a friend like silence
for the long journey left;
a shy boy, with voice interwoven
     enough to quiet all that quiet brings.
     to quiet all of me.

     stilling…everything.

     and i swear i hear a voiceless tune

     somewhere between me and you

     in the void avoided

     the echo true,

who knew,
silence
sings
too.

Meaning & Sound

Poems are made up of words that create meaning and sound. The sound of the word must be vocalized in mouth or in thought. That sound carries an innate meaning: an idea, experience or memory.

For example, a word like mug, for me, carries the *meaning* of a warm drink, friendship and reflection— arising from definition, but also from experience. Regarding *sound*, mug has a soft m, (mmm), and a long u, (uhhh), and a softer form of the letter g (gh rather then jee). Contrast "mug" to "cup." Though their meanings are close, cup has a shorter, sharper sound, a bit harsher, and ends with a sharp "p."

These word choices create the art and pleasure of poetry. Sound and meaning create a poet's canvas and words become paint in the reader's ear. To appreciate poetry, one needs to develop an appreciation for the innate palate of sound and meaning in everyday language[2].

---

[2] ideas for Meaning & Sound are borrowed from Mary Oliver, *A Poetry Handbook*'

Take a moment to consider:

- What words or phrases stand out in these poems?

- What word-sounds catch your ear?

- What is your sense of the author's meaning?

- What does each poem mean to you?

Experience, Mood & Emotion

Poets use the meaning and sounds of words to create a *mood* through our common experience. Take the phrase, "A tall, nonfat, triple-shot latte's ready at the bar." This everyday quip contains a lot of quick-sounding words, with clear meanings. For me, the mood of this phrase seems fast, direct, harsh, and even a bit impersonal. And for the poet, communicating that experience is central.

Poets paint with language through phrases and scenes that attempt to coax out common *experience*. The best poetry articulates the experience of the heart. Enjoyment, beauty, and connection grasp the reader when the poet enfleshes in language something true in the reader's experience. The words tap into our common humanity, communicating for the reader what before may have been inexpressible.

Mood carries with it an *emotion*. The phrase, "Come here, Darling," with its soft consonants and almost melodic sound can signify for many the comforting invitation of a caretaker. To me, it sounds like safety, peace, even touch. While reading, I may begin to feel a longing to be comforted or recall a memory of someone's tangible care. The descriptors one uses may differ from person to person, but the experience, the mood, the emotion remains as the locus of our formation.

Take a moment to consider:

- What common experience stands out to you in these poems? How would you describe the mood?

- What emotion do you think the poet is feeling? As you read, what are you feeling?

- Remember, the poet is writing about experience, so the meaning can remain largely relative without losing the meaning of that experience. It is important to consider what experience this poem surfaces for *you*.

Listening

Lastly, *listening* is the virtue cultivated through poetry. Learning to hear a poem at heart-level and receive nourishment from those words is a powerful activator for personal and relational growth.

This practice of poetical listening creates hospitality—the poem becomes a place where self-reflection, honesty, and emotion are welcome. Hospitality and its gifts can overflow into a rich, meaning-filled, integrated life, if only we take time to listen.

Take a moment to consider:

- What is most deeply resonating with *you* about these poems?

- What do these poems have to do with *your* life, who *you* are, who *you've* been, and who *you* are becoming?

- Share these insights with someone safe.

Poet's on Poetry

"Language is rich, and malleable. It is a living, vibrant material, and every part of a poem works in conjunction with every other part—the context, the pace, the diction, the rhythm, the tone—as well as the very sliding, floating, thumping, rapping sounds of it..."

   -Mary Oliver, *A Poetry Handbook*

"[Poetry] need not be just a fabric of printed words to be laboriously raveled out by students or critics, but is (or can be) written in a speakable and hearable language, the integrity of which begins and ends in the quality of its music."

   -Wendell Berry, *A Timbered Choir*

"I like to suspect more...when that great Imagination which in the beginning, for Its own delight and for the delight of men...had invented and formed the whole world of Nature, submitted to express Itself in human speech, that speech should sometimes be called poetry. For poetry too is a little incarnation, giving body to what had before been invisible and inaudible."

   -C. S. Lewis, *Reflections on the Psalms*

COMING SOON!

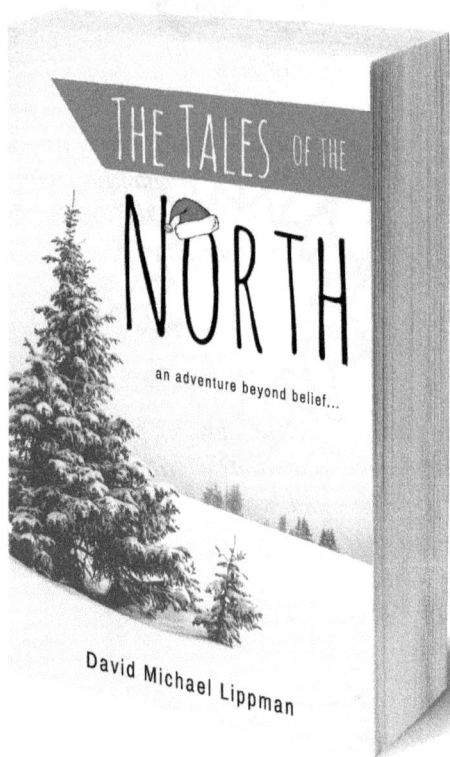

THE TALES OF THE

NORTH

an adventure beyond belief...

David Michael Lippman

Avery Thomas never believed Grandpa's crazy tales about the North. But when Grandpa and Mom are arrested without explanation, Avery, a fear-filled sophomore, and Holly, whom he secretly adores, are thrust into the hidden world of a corrupt North Pole. With swords readied, they must fly reindeer, fight elves, and find a way to keep Christmas and Avery's naïve younger sister alive.

JUST TURN THE PAGE!

DECEMBER BREAK

Avery Thomas stepped over piles of melting snow. A cold breeze blew over his shoulders toward Rutherford High School. Snow sloshed beneath his sneakers like mud.

Ugh.

He shook his foot, tightened his arms around his torso, and picked up his pace to keep off the cold.

December break had come faster than expected. Unlike other students, Avery wasn't looking forward to it. In fact, he wished that he could just fly through the Christmas season right into the New Year. He could really use a new year right now.

A black shape across the street caught his attention. Avery stopped.

He blinked hard. Something stood just right th—

A yellow school bus blew by. Its tires splashed a mud all over him, remnants of the first snowfall. Cold water stung and some even leaked through his jacket. Kids on the bus waved and laughed at him as it drove away.

Avery groaned and shook water off his arms. He glanced at the area across the road, it looked as dark and dreary as usual.

Great. Now he was seeing things.

He kicked a pile of wet leaves and they sloshed into the air. It didn't make him feel better. Shivering a little, he wiped the snot from his nose and hoped no one on the bus recognized him. He looked at the long stretch of road ahead of him. With each step Rutherford High loomed closer. Its large gray walls and old shingling reminded him of an oncoming storm. His breath floated into the cold air like smoke. If he'd learned anything at Rutherford, it's that no one likes sophomores.

❄

The hallways at Rutherford bustled with students shoving their jackets into lockers and grabbing piles of books for their classes. A few seniors huddled by a far locker, flocking around the cheerleaders. Cole, a tall tight end, held a girl in either arm.

Avery groaned. Football season was over. But they're still playing the same game.

10-15-22. Click. Avery shoved his black jacket into his locker and pulled out a history book that weighed more than he did. He also grabbed a Snickers bar from his stash—his favorite.

Click.

Three lockers down, he heard a familiar voice. Holly.

His chest tightened.

"Hey, Ave." She opened her locker, unwound her scarf, and pushed her maroon coat inside.

Avery slammed his locker hard and flinched at the bang.

"Hi, Hol." He stepped toward her, the history book weighing him down like an anchor. He'd known her since second grade. They were neighbors—nothing more.

"Aren't you excited for Christmas?" She smiled, her cheeks rosy. "I can't believe it's only a week away."

"Sure." Avery shrugged. He never understood why everyone got so excited. It was just another day.

"I love Christmas." Holly rubbed her hands together as if sitting by a roaring fire. "And snow, and the cold, and especially hot cocoa."

"Yeah, it's nice." Avery shrugged again. He didn't know if his teeth were chattering from the cold or something else.

"My family already set up our tree." Holly lifted the same history book as Avery's from her locker. She had already decorated it with a vibrant Christmas tree on the inside of the door smattered with funny cut-out ornaments—bands, clothes, nail polish, and other things only girls seemed to like.

"We always set it up the day after Thanksgiving. We get all the boxes down, my sis and I help Mom decorate the walls, and Dad puts up the lights. Then we all sit around the fire and tell stories." Her eyes lit up with holiday cheer. "Have you set up for Christmas yet?"

"Sort of." Avery pictured the piles of boxes, half-opened, around the undecorated Christmas tree in his living room. It looked more like moving day than a holiday. Sometimes he wished they really were moving. But then...

He looked up at Holly's bright green eyes.

"We should probably go," she said, "The bell already rang."

She turned down the hall, and Avery followed after her.

❄

"Quiet down," Mr. Reese shouted over the racket.

Holly and her friend Tasha, sitting in the front, stopped chatting and turned to the teacher. Avery took his seat at the second-to-last chair by the back window. Cole, in the opposite back corner, wouldn't stop talking to Vanessa.

Leaning his head on his arms, Avery waited for Mr. Reese to bark at Cole.

But Mr. Reese just sighed and began his lecture about ancient German fortifications.

Avery glanced out the window—the wind had picked up sending shivers across the grass fields on the school's south side. Humongous dark clouds stretched across the sky like the fingers of some winter god. Avery shuddered, imagining the storms of winter grasping at the throat of fall like a ferocious animal.

He stared. For a moment, he swore he saw something black move behind a tree. *What was...* He looked again. *No. Just a shadow.*

"Mr. Thomas?" said Mr. Reese. "Would you care to join us?"

Avery jerked forward. Out of the corner of his eye he could see Cole still whispering to Vanessa.

The whole class stared at him. Holly's concerned eyes met his.

"I...um," said Avery. "Sorry..."

"Good one, dork." Cole laughed in the back.

"Quiet, Mr. Burney." Mr. Reese pointed. "Unless you want to spend your first year of college in that very same desk."

"Too late," muttered Cole, but he still earned a few snickers nearby.

"Avery, *please* pay attention." Mr. Reese rubbed his forehead. "We need to get through this unit before Christmas, or else you won't be prepared for the PSATs."

"Yeah," Cole interjected. "As in Pathetically-Stupid Avery Thomas!"

Vanessa laughed.

"That's strike two, Mr. Burney." Mr. Reese held up two fingers. "Just continue with that attitude and you'll be spending Christmas in detention."

The whole class laughed. But Cole glared at Avery. Avery just sank deeper into his chair.

Mr. Reese shook his head and continued lecturing.

❅

Avery watched Holly get on the bus as he zipped up his jacket. The clouds above blackened. He walked a bit quicker, trying to catch Holly before—

The school bus pulled away with a puff of black smoke.

He gave a small wave, hoping Holly saw him. But he knew she didn't. *No one really does.*

"Hey, Thomas!" a rough voice shouted behind him.

Avery didn't turn around. He knew who it was.

Something hit him in the back of the head and Avery fell. A football rolled beside him.

"Turn around when I call you, Thomas," shouted Cole. A trail of teammates walked behind him, and a few popular cheerleaders followed, too.

As Avery tried to stand, Cole pushed him over with his foot. Avery stumbled to the ground again.

Cole laughed. "Get up."

"Yeah, get up!" another football player taunted as cheerleaders giggled.

Avery scooted and stood quickly, keeping his eyes on the ground. He tried to turn and walk away.

"Don't you walk away from me, *boy*." Cole yanked Avery close and whispered. "You made a fool of me in class today. No one messes with me, Thomas. Got that?"

Avery looked up at Cole's white face. His gray-black eyes burned with fire. Cole gripped both hands under Avery's shoulders, hefted him into the air, and hurled him to the ground again.

Avery slammed onto his backpack, and the book corners jabbed his ribs.

He groaned.

Cole picked up a thick tree branch and loomed over Avery.

Avery covered his head.

"If I that ever happens again, Thomas—" Cole lifted the branch with both hands. "—I'll snap you in half."

Cole collapsed the branch over his knee. It shattered pieces onto Avery like shrapnel.

Avery got up and ran.

He didn't turn to see if Cole chased him. He didn't even think to breathe. It didn't matter that his legs began to burn. Or that he'd left his cap on the ground where Cole clocked him. Or that Holly had glided away on the bus.

Nothing did. He slowed down as he turned the corner, his lungs gasping for air.

The long stretch of road lay out before him like the season of December. He sighed.

And it's just getting started.

THE ELVEN COUNCIL

Fire crackled in the ice caves of the North Pole as Kris Kringle awaited his trial. His elbows rested on the Northern Court's aged maple-wood table. He surveyed the gathering as the elf clans found their representative seats. Even in mid-July, hundreds had gathered for the emergency Elven Council—a rare feat, especially during the Pre-Distribution season.

Two miner elves stood guarding him with grimaces on their faces and long, sharp ice picks in their hands. But they didn't dare look at him.

Firelight flickered from the central hearth, casting strange shadows on the walls. Kris rubbed his large, calloused hands together. Traces of ancient coal from the mines darkened the creases on his fingers and palms.

He pulled a long pipe out of his shirt pocket, engraved with his sleigh and eight tiny reindeer.

Toymaker elves chattered and cast glances at him. Kris smirked at the elves. They turned quickly away.

He struck a match.

"Order. *Order*," called an elf's voice. The clans quieted.

Kris puffed 'til smoke spiraled out like a chimney in winter. Placing both hands behind his head, he leaned back and waited for the hordes of elves to decide his fate.

He couldn't help but chuckle. "This is what Christmas has come to?" Kris took a deep draw on his yuletide pipe. "So begins the war between elves and men."

Knewl, Kris's second in command and Chief of Toymakers, stood before the clans. Behind him, hundreds of elf eyes leered at Kris. Knewl spun around, pointing his scepter at him.

"Nothing like this has happened for centuries, Mr. Kringle. You should be ashamed of yourself. We elves will not live in ignorance. We will not stand by and watch while you undermine our welfare, our dignity."

Fire glowed behind Knewl's coal-dark eyes. Light from the fire glinted off his scepter, intricately carved with designs of blue, white, and gold and a sapphire set in the middle.

"You yourself have made holiday rulings in this very room, and it is by those very values we judge you tonight. It is a cruel world, even for an Old Saint like you. But this if you continue to reject to our laws, the Elven Council will not hesitate to condemn you actions and seek apt retribution for Christmas and the North."

Small elf hands applauded. Behind the clans, the last few elves stumbled in from the frosty night—old ones with long, pointy noses like witches and wrinkles that made their faces look like wooden carvings. Elf-sages.

The old, iron clad doors slammed shut.

Kris fiddled with a roll of old paper in his pocket then leaned forward on the table, staring at Knewl. He took another deep draw on his pipe and let the smoke leak from the side of his mouth. The Northern air stung his nose, and it felt rosy as ever.

"Bah," he whispered. "You know little of Christmas, Knewly."

Knewl glared at Kris.

All the elves kept watching Santa Claus.

He pulled the pipe from his mouth, smiled, and glanced at the bannered walls, robed with the reds and greens of Christmas. The colorful hats and garb of the clans dotted the room like ornaments on a tree. It seemed familiar and foreign, all at once.

Smoke circled his head like a wreath. He twirled his fingers through a lock of his long white beard, chuckled, and began to speak.

"Knewl, your coat fits nice, hmm?" Kris smirked. "I gave it to you three Christmases ago, did I not?"

Knewl yanked the coat higher on his shoulders. Kris meant to remind Knewl of the cold winters of their past. Knewl wouldn't quickly forget those conversations, when they'd dreamt of a better world for the North and its children.

"I knew what fit you then, and I know now. Put away your accusations, and leave the scepter alone."

"Do you *mock* me, Mr. Kringle?" Knewl's voice

shrilled. "You underestimate the elves. We are as old as the clay from which you were formed. We know what the Spirit of Christmas means for the North and for the world. We would give *everything* for Christmas's sake. Even if you will not—"

"You misunderstand, Knewl," Kris said. "If only you'd listen. You fear the North's fading glory. You fear a Christmas where children are present-less. You fear for the homes of your kin and the longstanding treaty between elves and men."

Kris tapped the end of his pipe on the table. Ashes scattered out and drifted away in the cavernous breeze. He placed the pipe back in his mouth and spoke around it. "These fears are well and good—but you know not the worst of fears. If you did, oh friend, you would hear me."

"I have heard you. *We* have heard you." Knewl paced quicker and quicker, brandishing the scepter like a broadsword in battle. "Year after year, you have carried the burden, Mr. Kringle. And we are grateful. But we see clearly now that the burden of Christmas was too much for you.

"You have forged this heretical path alone. You have become a threat to yourself and to the North. You must to surrender to our stipulations or be expelled from the North and from Christmas forever. Now you must understand—"

Kris slammed his fist onto the table. "No, Knewl, Son of Yningle, Chief of the Toymakers."

The whole room of elves trembled.

Kris continued, "This is neither about the North nor

about Christmas but about your own interest. If you stand against me, you stand against Christmas. You stand against the children. Listen to reason: there is a crisis of Christmas, and I am *not* it."

He opened his arms as if he were holding the whole world of children. "If you banish me, you will not fix your problem. It will only worsen. By your actions, the gift of Christmas will rot and fall to pieces. By your delay, threads of Christmas comfort are already unraveling like the ragged sweaters its patrons wear. Can you not see this?"

"I see fine, Mr. Kringle. And all I see is folly and foolishness as thick-headed as a wayward elven youth." Knewl lowered the scepter to the ground. Desperation gleamed in his eye. "With your words and actions, you condemn yourself. Your questions, your doubts, your ambitions violate the *laws* of the North. This you know well." Knewl turned to his fellow elves. "Brothers, bring forward the laws."

Elf hands clapped like pouring rain.

A bent-over elf Sage, one of those who examined the Scrolls, shuffled forward. He reached Knewl and presented him with an old, dry parchment rolled and tied with red and green twine.

Knewl bowed to him as if honoring a grandfather.

"Thank you, Estello." He turned again to his audience. "Hear, all, from the law of the elves." Knewl unrolled the scroll and began to read.

In accordance with the ancient tradition of the elves, all who threaten to debilitate, dispute, or destroy Christmas, elf or man, citizen or leader, must be judged before an Elven Council. If they do not repent of their deeds and confess their allegiance to Christmas and its traditions, as written in the scrolls of the Winter Solstice of our forefathers, upon which the eternal Saph-Fire burns, they then must face the punishment of the Chief Toymaker, in accordance with the heinous deed, as the council sees fit.

"Mr. Kringle," Knewl curled the scroll, turned to his audience and then back to Kris, "This council finds you guilty of threatening the traditions and perseverance of Christmas. You hold your questions and doubts as legitimate grounds for pursuing for the true meaning of Christmas. This is lunacy! " Knewl waved an arm in the air. "We *know* the meaning. We have always known. You, most of all, have *always* known. Or have you forgotten the thousands of years' elves served you loyally, without restraint?"

Knewl glowered.

"No. No, I dare say you have not forgotten—Santa Claus does not forget. But in defiance you have forged ahead, utterly denying the values which have founded Christmas and the Northern Empire. These trepidations, which you have shared with me in the privacy of your own home, have become overwhelming.

"I found no other recourse than to share them with the council, and with the North. Else your folly guide the North away from the ancient path millions have travelled to warmth of the fireside at Yuletide. Your questions corrode the fellowship of elves and men. You have consider neither the welfare of our cities nor our peace. You will destroy us all, along with all that is good about Christmas and the North. This is treachery, old saint. And we condemn your quest as a vain pursuit of *human*-kind."

As Knewl spoke, applause thundered from the elf clans. A few shouted and cajoled Kris.

"He's going to ruin our city!" yelled a toymaker.

"The old fool's threatening the coal trade!" A stout miner shook his arm.

"He's gone off the deep end!" A captain of the Skyfarers grimaced as tightly as his uniform and slick beret.

Kris drummed his fingertips on the wooden table, just waiting.

Knewl held up his hands, and the elves quieted. "Given the immediate pressures of the Northern cities and those abroad who serve Christmas loyally and depend on the season's prosperity, by no means can we simply watch as you dismantle our history and our welfare. We have sent detailed explanations of your offenses to the elven families of the North. What say you, Mr. Kringle? Will you relent? Won't you keep the peace between our people?"

Kris didn't answer Knewl's reading with his voice but with the rustling of another paper in his hands.

Whispers hissed among the elves seated around him.

Smoke drifted upward from the smoldering ashes of Kris's pipe.

"That is all well and good. But there is more to the *magic* of Christmas than your Elven traditions." He unrolled the scroll till it spanned the length of the table. "If you will not listen to reason, then maybe you and your council will listen to this."

The fire burned low. A cold wind arose. The room grew frigid as Kris raised the parchment. Shadows loomed. All sounds froze into silence.

Even Knewl lowered his legal parchment. All eyes fell on Kris.

"The list! The list!" Elven voices whispered around him.

Kris knew that some would be appalled that he would bring it here. Others would wonder if their names were marked in red. He could see them shuddering in their elven chairs. One slipped out into the cavernous night.

Knewl's grip tightened on the scepter, but soon all fell silent.

Kris untied the ornate knot and slowly unrolled the scroll. He cleared his throat and began to read. "Finnerly. *Naughty*. Raven. *Naughty*. Talti. *Naughty*…"

His eyes met with Knewl's. "Knewl. *Naughty*…"

ABOUT THE AUTHOR

David is a poet at heart, writing stories and devotional poetry for over 15 years. He has always delighted in the sounds and meanings of words mingling together, moving the soul as a symphony. For David, poetry is a place of discovery where he can express his heart while deepening and growing his relationship with God. David and his wife, Keri, live in the Santa Cruz Mountains. She more than anyone in his life has encouraged him toward the journey of writing. He couldn't have done this without her.

If you enjoy these poems please visit:
DavidMichaelLippman.com

Facebook.com/DavidMichaelLippman

@David_Michael_Lippman

www.ingramcontent.com/pod-product-compliance
Lightning Source LLC
Chambersburg PA
CBHW071928020426
42331CB00010B/2778